WHAT'S NEXT?

STUDY GUIDE | FIVE SESSIONS

THE JOURNEY TO
KNOW GOD, FIND FREEDOM,
DISCOVER PURPOSE,
& MAKE A DIFFERENCE

Chris Hodges

NELSON
BOOKS

An Imprint of Thomas Nelson

Contents

Introduction

> The only guarantee that tomorrow is going to get better is if you are growing today. And the most important growth for you and me is our spiritual growth, our walk with God.

> JOHN C. MAXWELL

Forrest Gump once declared that "life is like a box of chocolates... you never know what you're gonna get." As a pastor, I have encountered many people who seem to navigate their spiritual lives that way. They don't know where they're going, what they want to get, or even where they want to go. They know something is missing—and they long for a clearer sense of purpose and direction—but they just can't seem to find it.

Others I have encountered have been on a spiritual journey at a comfortable pace for most of their lives... so comfortable, in fact, they feel caught in a rut, spinning their wheels in a life that feels predictable and even boring. They, too, long for a deeper meaning in life, a deeper joy, a deeper connection to the God they love and the Savior they are committed to following. But they don't know where to turn or how to step off the treadmill they are on.

Some people are simply exhausted. Perhaps a major detour has left them reeling—a health crisis, divorce, or job loss has rerouted them from the path they once thought their lives would follow. They know God has a plan for them and have caught glimpses of where he wants them to go. But after being sidelined, they're tired and not sure how to get going again.

It may seem like a cliché, but we are all on a journey. At some point, we will all hit hills and valleys, twists and turns, intersections and detours that will cause to ask, "Now what? Which way do I go? *What's next* for my life?" During these crossroads moments, we need to pause and remember our priorities. We need to look beyond what's logical or convenient or advantageous. We need to look to God as our ultimate GPS, our soul's true compass, so we can lead a life that's purposeful, joyful, and significant for eternity.

This is why I wrote *What's Next?* and created this accompanying small-group study. During the course of the next five weeks, we will look at what it takes to get started on our journey with Christ and then take the next steps to *know God, find freedom, discover our purpose,* and ultimately *make a difference in our world.*

Now, this is not to say that I've got it all figured out. But I know the One who does—and you can know him as well. If your faith journey is just beginning, don't worry, because you won't get lost in these pages. If you're a mature believer who has been walking with Christ for a while now, there is still plenty for you. No matter where you are on your journey, this study will serve as a spiritual field guide to help you discover *what's next!*

How to Use This Guide

Group Size

The *What's Next?* video-based study is designed to be experienced in a group setting such as a Bible study, Sunday school class, or other small-group gathering. If the gathering is large, your leader may split everyone into smaller groups of five or six people to make sure everyone has enough time to participate in discussions.

Materials Needed

Everyone in your group will need his or her own copy of this study guide, which includes the opening questions you will discuss, notes for the video segments, directions for activities and discussion questions, and personal studies in between sessions. You will also want a copy of the *What's Next?* book, which provides further insights into the material you are covering in this study. (See the note at the end of each week's personal study for specific chapters to read in the book to prepare for the next week's group meeting.)

Facilitation

Your group will need to appoint a person to serve as a facilitator. This person will be responsible for starting the video and keeping track of time during discussions and activities. Facilitators may also ready questions aloud and monitor discussions, prompting participants to respond and ensuring that everyone has the opportunity to participate. If you have been chosen for this role, note there are additional instructions and resources in the back of this guide to help you lead your group members through the study.

Personal Studies

During the week, you can maximize the impact of the course with the personal studies provided for each session. You can treat each personal study section like a devotional and use them in whatever way works best for your schedule. You could do one section each day for three days of the week or complete them all in one sitting.

START THE JOURNEY

We need to look to God as our ultimate GPS,
our soul's true compass, if we want to live a life that's
purposeful, joyful, and significant for eternity.

CHRIS HODGES

Getting Started

Sometimes, the most difficult part of a journey is the first step. Perhaps you can relate. Maybe there is a place in the world you have been longing to visit. You've thought about how great it would be when you finally made it there. But try as you might, you just can't seem to figure out how to take the next step to make that trip a reality.

Or maybe the issue is you were hit with setbacks when you tried to make plans. You realized that to afford the trip, you wouldn't be able to stay in all the quaint Bed & Breakfasts you envisioned. Or the weather at the time you could travel wasn't ideal. Or a family commitment arose . . . and you couldn't see how to take some time off for a vacation.

We can come up with any number of reason as to why we can't pursue a goal. The same was true of the people in Jesus' day. The crowds had heard about Jesus' teachings and his miracles, and many wanted to follow him. But not all could find the time or the willingness to step away from their obligations. Luke describes some of these people in his Gospel:

> On the road someone asked if he could go along. "I'll go with you, wherever," he said. Jesus was curt: "Are you ready to rough it? We're not staying in the best inns, you know."
>
> Jesus said to another, "Follow me." He said, "Certainly, but first excuse me for a couple of days, please. I have to make arrangements for my father's funeral." Jesus refused. "First things first. Your business is life, not death. And life is urgent: Announce God's kingdom!"
>
> Then another said, "I'm ready to follow you, Master, but first excuse me while I get things straightened out at home." Jesus said, "No procrastination. No backward looks. You can't put God's kingdom off till tomorrow. Seize the day" (Luke 9:57–62 MSG).

As you look at your life, is there something that is keeping you from *seizing the* day? Is there something that is holding you back? If so, it's time to identify those obstacles in your life. In this first lesson, we will look at some common obstacles that get in the way of our journey with Christ and determine how we can move past them.

Opening Discussion

For this first session, go around the group and introduce yourselves to one another, and then answer the following questions:

- When was the last time you got lost while on a road trip? How did you end up getting back on track?

- What made you want to be a part of this group? What are you hoping to get out of this study?

Video Teaching

Play the video segment for session 1. As you watch, use the following outline to record any thoughts, questions, or points that stand out to you.

Notes

God wants you to know him, find freedom, discover your purpose, and make a difference

Three things you need to move on from include:

Old history

Old habits

Old hurts

Write down this phrase: *"I can't start* _____ *"*

It's time to *repent*—to change your mind and your direction in these areas:

It's time to get closer to God

It's time to get honest with a friend

It's time to get in tune with your purpose and passions

It's time to get doing something greater than yourself

If you dedicate your life to something greater than yourself, God will fill your life with passion and adventure

Group Discussion

Take a few minutes with your group members to discuss what you just watched and explore these concepts in Scripture.

1. At a traffic light, you might have to give the car in front of you a "beep beep" to get them moving. How has God done this in your life when he wanted you to move forward?

2. In Luke 9:57–62, many people wanted to follow Jesus, but they had all kinds of excuses why they could not. What are areas where you are prone to procrastinate in your spiritual life?

3. Read Isaiah 43:18–19. What does it mean to "forget" the former things in your life? How can being locked in the past prevent you from moving forward?

4. Read 2 Corinthians 5:17–18. What are some old habits and old hurts that you need put behind you in order to step into the new life that God has for you?

5. What are some things that tend to get in the way of you getting closer to God? Of getting honest with others? Of getting in tune with your passions in life?

6. Read Ephesians 2:10. What is the "work" that you feel God is calling you to do? What first step will you take this week to start moving toward that calling?

Individual Activity

Close out today's session by completing this short activity on your own.

1. Briefly review the video outline and any notes you took.

2. In the space below, write down the most significant point you took away from this session—from the teaching, activities, or discussions.

What I want to remember from this session is . . .

Closing Prayer

Go around the room and share any prayer requests you would like the group to pray about. Conclude your session by praying for these requests together. Ask God to work in each of your hearts throughout the week as you reflect on all you have covered during this first meeting.

If you haven't already started reading Chris Hodges's field guide for spiritual growth and transformation in *What's Next?*, now is a great time to begin. This week, read the introduction to the book before doing this study. The questions and exercises provided in this section are designed to help you receive the greatest benefit from reading the book and applying it to your own life. There will be time for you to share your reflections and results at the beginning of the next session.

Reflect

Most maps and online GPS apps include an indication of your present location. Whether it's "you are here" on the diagram of the amusement park or "present location" on your phone or tablet, these starting points help you get your bearings and prepare for your journey. As you begin this study, consider how you would describe your current location on your journey of faith. Use the following questions to help you think about where you are right now in life and in your relationship with God.

Do you see yourself as being closer to the beginning, middle, or end of your faith journey? Is your answer based on the amount of time you've known the Lord, the experiences you've encountered, or something else? Explain.

Is your present vantage point from a valley (low point) or from mountain summit (high point)? Or do you feel as though your path has plateaued and you've been on solid ground for a while?

What do you consider the greatest obstacles or biggest challenges to moving forward in your spiritual journey? How have these barriers hindered your progress in the past?

Within the four areas of growth, which one best describes your present focus? Knowing God as your loving Father? Finding freedom from old struggles, habits, and thought patterns? Discovering your purpose as you serve God and advance his kingdom? Making a difference for eternity as you invest your time, treasure, and talents in God's purposes? Explain.

On a scale of 1 to 10, with 1 being "far away" and 10 being "very close," how would you rate where you are in proximity to God? Why did you choose this score? Where would you *like* to be in your relationship with God?

. . . .

God is the only one who can know you at your deepest levels. He made you and knows the purpose for which you were designed. He alone holds the book on your life and knows the number of your days. You can never find fulfillment and true, lasting joy apart from knowing him. You cannot begin to know what step to take next in your life without him. Knowing God is the key to life.

WHAT'S NEXT? PAGES 7–8

. . . .

Dig Deeper

The opening of section 1, "Know God," in *What's Next?* includes several verses that focus on what it means to accept Jesus as your Lord and Savior, welcome his Holy Spirit into your life, and grow in your relationship with God. Read through the following passages and identify what they mean to you about knowing God at this point in your life.

> *Jesus answered, "I am the way and the truth and the life. No one comes to the Father except through me"* (John 14:6).

Behold, I stand at the door and knock; if anyone hears My voice and opens the door, I will come in to him (Revelation 3:20 NKJV).

If you declare with your mouth, "Jesus is Lord," and believe in your heart that God raised him from the dead, you will be saved. For it is with your heart that you believe and are justified, and it is with your mouth that you profess your faith and are saved (Romans 10:9–10).

Salvation is found in no one else, for there is no other name under heaven given to mankind by which we must be saved (Acts 4:12).

But to all who believed him and accepted him, he gave the right to become children of God (John 1:12 NLT).

Can you think of other passages from God's Word that help you understand your relationship with him? List them below along with a brief indication of how they speak to you.

. . . .

[Knowing God] is a recurring process of walking with God throughout your life. It's an ongoing dynamic relationship, a process of
continuing to know each other longer and deeper, closer and closer.
If you marry someone, your marriage doesn't end after the ceremony
or on your first, second, tenth, or golden wedding anniversary. It's an
ongoing dynamic relationship, a process of continuing to know each
other longer and deeper, closer and closer. Knowing God is quite
similar. You can know his voice by praying, talking, and listening to
him. You can know his ways by reading, studying, and applying them.

WHAT'S NEXT?, PAGE 8

. . . .

Identify

Across the centuries, followers of Jesus have cultivated habits that
help them know God at a deeper level. Sometimes called "spiritual
disciplines," these practices can help provide structure and conti-
nuity within your daily and weekly schedule so you can make your
time with God a practical priority. You may have enjoyed using
some of these practices in the past, or you may be discovering
them for the first time. Either way, they can enhance the quality
of time spent praying, reading the Bible, or serving others.

On the following page is a brief, non-comprehensive list of
several spiritual practices. Place a checkmark next to the one that
you will commit to pursue between now and when your group
next meets . . . and then continue to practice it until your group
completes this study. Consider choosing a spiritual practice you
have never tried before to see how it helps you know God in a new
or different way. If you're not sure, spend a few moments in prayer
and ask the Holy Spirit to guide you.

- ❏ **Praying daily**—for at least ten minutes each day or up to thirty minutes
- ❏ **Taking a prayer walk**—around your neighborhood, through your community, in the beauty of nature, alone or with others
- ❏ **Reading your Bible daily**—on your own or using a Bible study guide
- ❏ **Memorizing Scripture**—a strategic verse or passage that speaks to where you are right now
- ❏ **Meditating on a Bible verse or passage**—asking the Holy Spirit to guide you
- ❏ **Reflecting on a key word or phrase from Scripture**— in silence for at least five minutes
- ❏ **Volunteering to serve others**—at a homeless shelter, food bank, or mentoring program
- ❏ **Volunteering to serve at your church**—two hours a week, or whatever is needed
- ❏ **Preparing a meal for someone in need**—in your neighborhood, church, community, or workplace

. . . .

[God is] speaking to your heart, pursuing you, wooing you, gently and persistently knocking on your door and waiting for your response. "Behold, I stand at the door and knock. If anyone hears My voice and opens the door, I will come in to him" (Revelation 3:20 NKJV). If you're already in a relationship with God and have opened your heart to Jesus, then it's time to find out what's next on your journey; it's time to experience the joy, peace, and purpose you can know as you grow in your faith.

WHAT'S NEXT?, PAGE 12

. . . .

Take a Step

As you think back over your first group meeting, as well as how God has spoken to you through your time alone with him this week, consider what you want to get out of this study. Create a map, diagram, flow chart, or mood board that shows where you are right now and where you want to be by the time you complete this study. Have fun and make it your own, with colorful markers, magazine photos, and other materials that inspire you. Keep your focus on illustrating the spiritual journey you would like to make during the next few weeks as you read *What's Next?*, meet with your group, and complete this study. If you'd like, bring it to your group next week and share your vision! Be sure hold on to it until you've completed this study.

In preparation for session 2, read the opening for section 1, "Know God," and chapters 1–3 in *What's Next?* Use the space below to note any key points or questions you want to share at the beginning of your next group meeting.

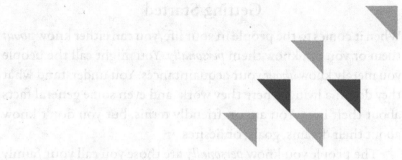

SESSION 2

KNOW GOD

Wherever you are, whatever you're going through, the fuel for your spiritual journey comes from a real, dynamic, personal, close relationship with the living God.

CHRIS HODGES

Getting Started

When it comes to the people in your life, you can either know *about* them or you can know them *personally*. You might call the people you merely know *about* your acquaintances. You understand what they do for a living, where they work, and even some general facts about their lives. You are on friendly terms, but you don't know about their dreams, goals, or desires.

The people you know *personally* are those you call your family and friends. You know what makes them happy, what makes them angry, what they like, what they can't stand . . . basically, everything about what makes them tick. You like to spend time with these people and feel your life is better because they are in it.

A story told in the Gospel of Luke reveals the type of relationship that Jesus wants to have with us. It begins in the city of Jericho, where a chief tax collector named Zacchaeus had learned Jesus would be passing through the town. Luke tells us what happens next:

> *Zacchaeus . . . wanted desperately to see Jesus, but the crowd was in his way—he was a short man and couldn't see over the crowd. So he ran on ahead and climbed up in a sycamore tree so he could see Jesus when he came by.*
>
> *When Jesus got to the tree, he looked up and said, "Zacchaeus, hurry down. Today is my day to be a guest in your home." Zacchaeus scrambled out of the tree, hardly believing his good luck, delighted to take Jesus home with him* (Luke 19:2–6 MSG).

Zacchaeus wanted to know more *about* Jesus, so he went to great lengths to climb a tree to catch a glimpse of Christ. But Jesus wanted to know Zacchaeus *personally,* so he called up as he was passing by and invited himself to dinner at Zacchaeus's house. Jesus wants us to know him and have a *personal* relationship with him. As he said to his disciples, "I no longer call you servants . . . instead, I have called you friends" (John 15:15).

In this session, we will look at what it means to know God personally . . . and what we can do to take the next steps to get closer to him.

Opening Discussion

If you or any of your group members are meeting for the first time, take a few minutes to introduce yourselves. Next, go around the group and answer the following questions:

- What is the difference between doing a task out of a sense of duty as opposed to doing a task out of a sense of devotion to something or someone?

- Looking back at your notes, what stood out to you in your between-sessions studies that you would like to share with the group?

Video Teaching

Play the video for session 2. As you watch, use the following outline to record any thoughts, questions, or points that stand out to you.

Notes

The two trees in Eden indicate the two approaches you can take to try to be godly:

Try to be godly through knowledge (the Tree of Knowledge)

Try to be godly through a relationship with God (the Tree of Life)

Three ways you can stay close to God and have a real relationship with him:

Focus on loving Jesus

Focus on the relationship, not the rules

Guard your heart from going back

Approach God out of *delight* instead of *duty*

Group Discussion

Take a few minutes with your group members to discuss what you just watched and explore these concepts in Scripture.

1. How would you describe your approach when it comes to reading the Bible and spending time with God in prayer? Do you view it a discipline or a delight?

2. In Genesis 2:8–9, God planted two trees in Eden, which represent two different ways of approaching him. What type of approach does the *Tree of Knowledge* represent? What is the problem with approaching God only in this way?

3. What type of approach to God does the *Tree of Life* represent? Of the two different approaches, which describes the way you tend to relate to God?

4. In John 14:15, Jesus said those who love him will keep his commands. How has a focus on loving Jesus led you to a greater desire to want to follow his commands?

5. Jesus challenged the religious leaders of his day because they focused on following God's law to the letter rather than on having a real relationship with him. As you look at your life, what are some ways you might be guilty of doing the same?

6. What are some effective ways you have found of maintaining your relationship with God? What changes have you seen in your life as a result?

Individual Activity

Close out today's session by completing this short activity on your own.

1. Briefly review the video outline and any notes you took.

2. In the space below, write down the most significant point you took away from this session—from the teaching, activities, or discussions.

What I want to remember from this session is . . .

Closing Prayer

Conclude this session by praying aloud together, thanking God for the many ways he has allowed you to get to know him better. Ask God to continually give you a desire to get to know him better out of a sense of devotion rather than out of duty. Also share any personal requests that you would like the group members to pray about during the week.

Similar to what you did after session 1, the following questions and exercises will help you apply this week's teaching and practice the personal application. Before you begin, make sure you have finished reading chapters 1–3 in *What's Next?* As you consider what it means to have a vibrant and living relationship with God, reflect on your responses and ask the Holy Spirit to guide you toward the next steps. There will be time for you to share your observations and outcomes at the beginning of the next session.

Reflect

Spend a few moments to quiet your heart before God and ask the Holy Spirit to help you make the most of this study time. Then use the following questions to help you reflect on the way you approach God and the relationship that you have with him.

What stands out most to you as you think about your last group session? How did your approach to knowing God change or shift?

After reading chapter 1 in *What's Next?*, how would you explain baptism to someone who is unfamiliar with the Christian faith? How is baptism similar to a wedding ring? Do you agree with the analogy? Why or why not?

If you have been baptized, how would you describe the event and its significance to you as a follower of Jesus? What did your baptism convey to your family, to your friends, and to others in your church community?

If you have not yet been baptized, what is holding you back? Do you have questions that linger about the meaning of baptism? If so, write them down below.

In addition to baptism, what are some other events, spiritual milestones, or special moments that have helped you know God at a deeper level? Has a particular retreat or conference been especially encouraging or revealing? What made that particular event special?

Looking ahead at the next month, plan a time when you can get away, either alone or with others, and focus on deepening your relationship with God.

. . . .

Just as marriage requires effort and commitment, our relationship with God requires us to follow through on making him our number-one priority. That means we have to find time to pray. If I tell my wife I love her but never have time to talk to her, she will begin to question the depth of my love and commitment. Similarly, we have to do more than just say we want to know God. We have to make time to talk with him and continue the conversation from day to day.

WHAT'S NEXT?, PAGES 26–27

. . . .

Dig Deeper

Most people, at one time or another, struggle in their prayer life. The cause might stem from misperceptions about how to pray, busy schedules, emotional responses to life circumstances, or a combination of all these factors.

But Jesus emphasized the need to talk with your heavenly Father on a regular basis if you want to experience his love and know the freedom that comes from depending on him. Sometimes, in order to grow in your prayer life, you will have to find new ways to pray even as you hold fast to the model Jesus gave us when his disciples asked him to teach them how to pray (see Luke 11:1).

Notice how Jesus' model prayer in Matthew 6:9–13 covers all the spiritual and relational areas you need for intimacy with God:

> *Our Father in heaven,*
> *Hallowed be Your name.*
> *Your kingdom come.*
> *Your will be done*
> *on earth as it is in heaven.*
> *Give us this day our daily bread.*
> *And forgive us our debts,*
> *as we forgive our debtors.*
> *And do not lead us into temptation,*
> *but deliver us from the evil one.*
> *For Yours is the kingdom and the power*
> *and the glory forever* (NKJV).

In chapter 2 of *What's Next?*, you will find a discussion of the parts of this model prayer that will help you understand how to incorporate them into your conversations with God. Spend a couple of minutes praying through each of these parts. Pause before going on to the next part of the prayer so you can listen to how God wants to speak to your heart.

- Connect with God relationally (*"our Father"*)
- Worship him (*"hallowed be your name"*)
- Focus on God's agenda first (*"your kingdom come"*)
- Request what we need today (*"give us today our daily bread"*)
- Ask for forgiveness for our sins and forgive others (*"and forgive us our debts"*)
- Protect us from the enemy (*"and lead us not into temptation"*)
- Praise God for his power and sovereignty (*"for yours is the kingdom"*)

. . . .

Scripture tells us, "Sovereign LORD, you have made the heavens and the earth by your great power and outstretched arm. Nothing is too hard for you" (Jeremiah 32:17). . . . Even when you don't feel victorious, remind yourself of the truth of God's Word. Don't let your emotions dictate how and when and why you pray. Talk to God. Open your heart. Listen to him. Praise him and give him thanks for all the blessings in your life. Praise him for who he is and how you are able to talk to him directly.

WHAT'S NEXT?, PAGES 37–38

. . . .

Identify

Whether you have been walking with God for only a few weeks or most of your life, you have undoubtedly experienced a number of changes in your goals and priorities. As you reflect today on what it means to *know*, think about a "before and after" snapshot of your life.

How would you describe your lifestyle, focus, goals, and direction before you asked Jesus into your life, accepted God's gift of grace, and committed to following him? What areas of your life probably did not please God or align with his instructions in the Bible?

After making the decision to enter into a personal relationship with God, how did your life change? Were these changes immediate or did they take a while? How did you discern what habits and behaviors pleased God and which did not?

As you have grown in your faith, what other aspects of your lifestyle have changed? What has caused those changes? (Consider everything that comes to mind: how you look, what you wear, who your friends are, your attitude, your habits and preferences, the kind of music you listen to or programs you watch, the way you surf online or follow social media . . . everything.)

What areas do you still wish to change so they are more aligned with pleasing God and following his will? What needs to happen in order to make those changes?

Whose lives have you seen change because of their relationship with God? What struck you most about the ways their attitude, language, and behavior changed? How has their spiritual growth inspired and encouraged your own?

. . . .

We sometimes make prayer harder than it has to be when really it is just talking with God. And the more you do it, the more comfortable and natural it feels. You don't have to use fancy words or English from the King James Version of the Bible. God isn't grading you on how well you communicate—in fact, there's nothing you can do to impress him. He simply wants to know your heart, to listen to you, to talk with you. . . . The key to prayer is to just do it!

WHAT'S NEXT?, PAGES 38–39

. . . .

Take a Step

"Very early in the morning, while it was still dark, Jesus got up, left the house and went off to a solitary place, where he prayed" (Mark 1:35).

Most of us say we want to make time to know God better and grow closer to him, but it often feels impossible to find uninterrupted time when we can quiet our souls and be still before him. Perhaps one reason we struggle is because we want to commit to spending that kind of focused time with him *each and every day*. Practically speaking, however, it might be easier to make a date with God once a week.

Before your next group meeting, set a time and date when you will unplug from online devices for at least an hour. Plan ahead where and how you will spend your time with God. You might consider getting up an hour earlier, lighting a candle, listening to praise music, and reading some of your favorite Psalms. Or you might simply want to spend your lunch hour in a park, opening your heart to God and listening to his voice in the midst of an otherwise busy day. You could also go on a longer walk in a beautiful setting after work or find an empty church or place of worship where you can enjoy spending special time alone with your God.

Whatever you choose, make it a priority to keep your appointment with God!

_____

In preparation for session 3, read the opening for section 1, "Find Freedom," and chapters 4–6 in What's *Next?* Use the space below to note any key points or questions you want to share at the beginning of your next group meeting.

SESSION 3

FIND FREEDOM

Every human being wants to be free, to enjoy the ability to choose
for themselves where and how they live out their lives. . . . It's in us
to be free—God put the longing there.

CHRIS HODGES

Getting Started

Growing up, you can probably remember a time when the kids at school were mean to you, teased you, or bullied you. Perhaps you shrugged it off as being "no big deal." But the truth is those experiences made an impact on you. If you have wounds you can't seem to get past or forgive, they could be holding you back from taking the next step in your journey with Christ.

In the Gospel of John, we read about a woman who had received many such wounds in her past. Jesus encountered her when he was traveling through the region of Samaria. She was surprised when Jesus addressed her, for Jewish men did not speak to women in public. Also, she was a *Samaritan*—a race hated by the Jews—and had obviously received scorn from other Jewish men in the past.

But there were other areas of relational wounding as well. The woman had been married five times and was living with a man who was not her husband. At the time, a woman could not initiate divorce except in rare cases, so it's likely the husbands had divorced her or died. Both would have been devastating losses and causes for her to receive judgment from others. But Jesus hadn't come to judge her. He had come to set her free. He said to her:

> *"It's who you are and the way you live that count before God. Your worship must engage your spirit in the pursuit of truth. That's the kind of people the Father is out looking for: those who are simply and honestly themselves before him in their worship"* (John 4:24 MSG).

Jesus wanted the woman to know God cared about her and accepted her in spite of her past. But he didn't want to just leave her there—he wanted to establish a relationship with her that would move her to the next steps in her journey. And unlike the other relationships she had experienced, God would never fail her or cause her harm.

God is still in the business of freeing people today. In this session, we will look at what he does to bring that freedom . . . and the part we have to play.

Opening Discussion

Go around the group and answer the following questions:

- What are some of your fondest memories from your past? How do you think those experiences have shaped your life today?

- Looking back at your notes, what stood out to you in your between-sessions studies that you would like to share with the group?

Video Teaching

Play the video segment for session 3. As you watch, use the following outline to record any thoughts, questions, or points that stand out to you.

Notes

Three things that will keep you from experiencing God's best for your life:

Your sin (and bad choices)

What others did to you

Your circumstances

Jesus talked about forgiveness in the Lord's Prayer

Terah's son Haran died in Ur of the Chaldeans

Terah couldn't move on from the city of Haran to get to where God wanted him to be

We need to "get out of Haran" and move past the relational wounds in our lives

Group Discussion

Take a few minutes with your group members to discuss what you just watched and explore these concepts in Scripture.

1. What are some choices in your life that you are glad you made? How do you think your life has been better as a result of making those wise decisions?

2. What are some choices in your life that you regret making? How do you think your life would be different today if you had taken a different course of action?

3. In 1 Peter 5:8, we are warned to be alert to the schemes of the devil. What are some ways the enemy has tried to attack you? How do you stay alert to his schemes?

4. In Matthew 6:12, Jesus told his disciples to ask God to forgive their sins just as they had forgiven those who had sinned against them. Why does forgiveness play such an important part in our ability to gain freedom from the wounds of the past?

5. In Genesis 11:31–32, Terah (the father of Abraham) was unable to move on from the city of Haran to the land where God wanted him to settle. What are some relational wounds in your past that you have found difficult to move on from? Why?

6. How do you think your life would change if you were willing to move on and forgive those people who wronged you? What do you see as your "Promised Land"?

Individual Activity

Close out today's session by completing this short activity on your own.

1. Briefly review the video outline and any notes you took.

2. In the space below, write down the most significant point you took away from this session—from the teaching, activities, or discussions.

What I want to remember from this session is . . .

Closing Prayer

Before you end with prayer, share one area of your life in which you want to experience more of God's freedom. You don't have to explain or describe your struggle, but let others know enough so they can pray specifically for your request. Begin your group prayer time by thanking God for the freedom you all have in Christ. Pray for each other's requests and claim the power of God over every burden that was shared. Conclude by asking God's Spirit to give each of you peace and keep you safe from the attacks of the enemy.

As you saw in the video teaching this week, you don't have to remain a prisoner of your past. Jesus died to set the *captives*—which is each of us—completely free. The enemy of your soul has no claim on your life! Before you begin this week's study, make sure you have read chapters 4–6 in *What's Next?* Again, there will be time for you to share your observations at the beginning of the next session.

Reflect

If you want to find freedom from the wounds of the past, the first place to begin is by *identifying* the issues, hurts, and past baggage that are weighing you down. Sometimes these weights will be front and center, and you feel as if you are well aware of what is holding you back. Other times, you think you have moved past an old offense only to have it sneak up on you and storm into your life again. Before answering the questions that follow, spend a few minutes in prayer, asking the Holy Spirit to guide you and to be with you.

What was your greatest takeaway from your group's last meeting? What did you learn from what others shared?

WHAT'S NEXT? STUDY GUIDE

What one issue, habit, relationship, or past event continues to limit your freedom to be all that God made you to be? What does it mean for you to surrender this area to God at this point in your journey?

How have you limited the way you see yourself, your life, and your relationship with God because of past mistakes and old baggage? What needs to happen for you to break free and begin, or continue, to live in the freedom you have through the power of God?

What habit or sinful behavior continues to bind you the most on your faith journey? How have you tried to address it? How can you experience God's freedom in this particular area?

What would your life look like if you were living in the fullness of God's freedom? How would you describe it? How would you feel differently than you do now?

....

Most of us are not bound as tightly as we think we are. Most of
our issues stem from the lies we've accepted as truth that cause us to
stay where we are, stuck in place, running on a treadmill of repetitive
negative thoughts that prevent us from moving forward in
God's freedom. We think there's nothing we can do to change—which
is true, we can't—but our God can! If you want to take the next step in
your spiritual growth, then it's time to break free from the chains that
bind you and the obstacles that continually seem to trip you up.

WHAT'S NEXT?, PAGE 62

....

Dig Deeper

If you want to live in freedom, you have to be grounded in the
truth. Facing the truth is not always easy or comfortable, but it is
the only way to grow closer to God and mature in your faith. Jesus
told his followers, "If you hold to my teaching, you are really my
disciples. Then you will know the truth, and the truth will set you
free" (John 8:31–32).

It is never easy to be honest about your mistakes, your secrets,
your flaws, and your sinful behaviors. But in order to receive God's
grace, peace, and joy, you have to let go of your fear, shame, and
anger. In the Bible, we read how King David knew he had disobeyed
God but couldn't come to terms with the fact he had committed
adultery with Bathsheba and had her husband, Uriah, killed to
cover up their sin (see 2 Samuel 11). Only after the prophet Nathan
rebuked him did the king confess before God and repent of his sin.

In Psalm 51, David expresses the cries of his heart after rec-
ognizing the depth of his transgression. As you read through this
passage, think about the one issue, person, wound, or struggle that
came to mind in the Reflect section. Make David's words the prayer

of your heart as you seek forgiveness, accept grace, and receive a fresh start in the freedom God gives you.

Have mercy on me, O God,
according to your unfailing love;
according to your great compassion
blot out my transgressions.
Wash away all my iniquity
and cleanse me from my sin.

For I know my transgressions,
and my sin is always before me.
Against you, you only, have I sinned
and done what is evil in your sight;
so you are right in your verdict
and justified when you judge.
Surely I was sinful at birth,
sinful from the time my mother conceived me.
Yet you desired faithfulness even in the womb;
you taught me wisdom in that secret place.

Cleanse me with hyssop, and I will be clean;
wash me, and I will be whiter than snow.
Let me hear joy and gladness;
let the bones you have crushed rejoice.
Hide your face from my sins
and blot out all my iniquity.

Create in me a pure heart, O God,
and renew a steadfast spirit within me.
Do not cast me from your presence
or take your Holy Spirit from me.
Restore to me the joy of your salvation
and grant me a willing spirit, to sustain me.

Then I will teach transgressors your ways,
so that sinners will turn back to you.
Deliver me from the guilt of bloodshed, O God,
you who are God my Savior,
and my tongue will sing of your righteousness.
Open my lips, Lord,
and my mouth will declare your praise.
You do not delight in sacrifice, or I would bring it;
you do not take pleasure in burnt offerings.
My sacrifice, O God, is a broken spirit;
a broken and contrite heart
you, God, will not despise.

May it please you to prosper Zion,
to build up the walls of Jerusalem.
Then you will delight in the sacrifices of the righteous,
in burnt offerings offered whole;
then bulls will be offered on your altar.

. . . .

Only God can forgive our sins, but confession takes care of what we did. It doesn't guarantee we won't mess up again. In fact, left to our own devices, most of us will fail time after time. But God provided a solution, a system that relies on our identity as relational beings. He said, "Therefore confess your sins to each other and pray for each other so that you may be healed" (James 5:16). We confess our sins not only to God but also to each other. This system provides spiritual support as we pray for each other and help each other, which facilitates healing. Notice the big picture here: we go to God for forgiveness, and we go to God's people for healing.

WHAT'S NEXT?, PAGE 71

. . . .

Identify

As you read in chapters 4–6 of *What's Next?*, it is essential to have godly relationships and be a part of Christian community if you desire to find freedom. How has God used other people to help you experience freedom from past wounds, present struggles, and future fears?

Who is your closest confidant—the person who knows more of you and your secrets than anyone else? How does he or she help you remember the truth of God's love, forgiveness, and mercy? (If you can't think of anyone like this in your life, ask God to guide you to a mature, trustworthy believer who would be willing hear your confession and pray with you.)

When has God used *you* to minister to someone else as that person has sought to grow in his or her spiritual freedom? How can you bless and encourage that person this week?

When was the last time that you had a heart-to-heart talk with a trusted friend and shared your present concerns and personal struggles? How did his or her response encourage you? Is it time to schedule another conversation to confess, challenge, and encourage each another?

What has been your experience with accountability within your close relationships? What does being accountable to another believer actually mean to you? How can accountability inspire, challenge, and encourage you rather than shame, condemn, and dishearten you?

. . . .

Everyone has been shaped by their relationships. Whether you realize it or not, you are the sum total of all the key relationships in your life up until now. All the more reason to pay close attention to your choice of friends. . . . Without a doubt, your relationships play a role in some of the most important decisions you'll ever make.

WHAT'S NEXT?, PAGES 72–73

. . . .

Take a Step

Make your relationships a priority this week as you seek to live in the freedom you have in Christ. Before your next group meeting, check in with at least one person from the group to see how he or she is doing. While you can send a text or email, try to find time for a call or, better yet, meet for a cup of coffee. Share with the person how you've been dealing with all that has come up in this week's exploration of spiritual freedom. Ask the person to pray for you and also ask how you can lift up his or her concerns. If possible, pray together before you finish your conversation.

In preparation for session 4, read the opening for section 3, "Discover Purpose," and chapters 7–9 in *What's Next?* Use the space below to note any key points or questions you want to share at the beginning of your next group meeting.

DISCOVER PURPOSE

God has a unique and distinct purpose for your life. He has
designed you specifically for the calling he has put on your life. . . .
You already have what it takes. You just have to unlock it!

CHRIS HODGES

Getting Started

You have undoubtedly, at some point in your life, heard about the importance of setting goals. You likely know the most effective goals are those that are *specific, measurable, attainable, relevant,* and *timely.* A well-established goal can help you know the correct course to take and the obstacles to avoid.

It's fun to dream big and imagine where life could lead several years down the road. But often, the problem you will find is that you set the *wrong* goals. As a result, you end up pursuing goals you thought would bring fulfillment . . . but only ended up leaving you empty and unsatisfied. This is why it is critical to have *God-honoring* dreams for your life.

A story told in Mark's Gospel reveals how Jesus had to help two of his disciples adjust their thinking and reset wrong goals. As the group made their way to Jerusalem, James and John began to dream about the positions they would hold in Jesus' kingdom. At one point, they asked Jesus to award them the highest places of honor. To this, Jesus replied:

> *"You've observed how godless rulers throw their weight around . . . and when people get a little power how quickly it goes to their heads. It's not going to be that way with you. Whoever wants to be great must become a servant. Whoever wants to be first among you must be your slave. That is what the Son of Man has done: He came to serve, not to be served—and then to give away his life in exchange for many who are held hostage"* (Mark 10:42–45 MSG).

In time, the disciples would come to understand that if they wanted to be elevated in God's kingdom, they needed to lower themselves and serve others. As they did this, they discovered a greater purpose than they had ever imagined. By taking the focus off themselves, they were able to fulfill Jesus' command to "go and make disciples of all nations, baptizing them in the name of the Father and of the Son and of the Holy Spirit" (Matthew 28:19).

In this session, we will look at the types of dreams that God wants us to have for our lives . . . and how following his guidance will lead us to finding our true purpose.

Opening Discussion

Check in with everyone by answering the following questions:

- What were some of the dreams you had for your life when you were a child? How many of those dreams came true for you?

- Looking back at your notes, what stood out to you in your between-sessions studies that you would like to share with the group?

Video Teaching

Play the video for session 4. As you watch, use the following outline to record any thoughts, questions, or points that stand out to you.

Notes

You have a God who is active and speaks to you today

Dreams are one of the means God uses to speak to his people

There are five types of people when it comes to dreams:

The person who has no dream

The person who has a wrong dream

The person who has a stale dream

The person who has a vague dream

The person who has a God-honoring dream

The harvest is plentiful . . . but the workers are few

Group Discussion

Take a few minutes with your group members to discuss what you just watched and explore these concepts in Scripture.

1. In Acts 2:17, Peter referred to a prophecy from the book of Joel to explain the events taking place on the Day of Pentecost. What did Peter say would happen in the "last days"? What are some of the ways that God communicates with us?

2. What are the characteristics of a person with *no dream* or with a *dream that died*? When in your life have you gone through a season in which you had no dream?

3. What are the characteristics of a person with the *wrong dream*? Has God ever revealed to you that you were chasing the wrong dream? What did you do as a result?

4. What does it mean to have a *stale dream*? What are some ways that you have "kept the fire going" when you had a dream that was ready to die?

5. What is the problem with having a *vague dream*? How have you given shape and substance to the dreams you are pursuing so they don't fall into this category?

6. What is the greatest *God-honoring dream* that you are currently pursuing? What challenges have you faced? What rewards have you seen for your efforts?

Individual Activity

Close out today's session by completing this short activity on your own.

1. Briefly review the video outline and any notes you took.

2. In the space below, write down the most significant point you took away from this session—from the teaching, activities, or discussions.

What I want to remember from this session is . . .

Closing Prayer

Go around the room and share any prayer requests you would like the group to pray about, and then pray for those requests together. Conclude by praying aloud, thanking God for the uniqueness of each person in the room and the dreams that he has given. Ask that God would help the group to pursue those dreams that honor him and matter for all eternity.

BETWEEN·SESSIONS
PERSONAL STUDY

As you saw in the video teaching this week, it is important to have big dreams—but it is absolutely critical that those big dreams honor God and represent his will for your life. Before you begin this week's study, make sure you have read chapters 7–9 in *What's Next?* The questions and exercises that follow will help you explore the unique gifts, abilities, and talents that God has given you and how you can use them to discover your purpose. Be sure to record your reflections and observations in this study guide so that you can share them with your group at the beginning of the next session.

Reflect

Today, take a few moments to look back on your life and how you have ended up doing what you are doing now. Ask the Holy Spirit to open your eyes and heart to help you discover a clearer sense of how God made you and what he wants you to do with your life. Use the questions below to assist in your reflection.

Do you know your divine purpose? Have you discovered what God placed inside you to share with others? If so, what is that purpose?

What gives you the most joy in life? When do you feel most alive, excited, and eager to serve? How have you found this personal passion to be related to God's purpose in your life?

Complete the following sentences as specifically as possible:

My purpose in life is . . .

I know this because . . .

In addition to your passions, pursuits, and personality, God will often use your experiences to reinforce your purpose and equip you for future service. What experiences in your life has God used to shape your purpose for his kingdom?

When have you endured a disappointment, frustrating conflict, or devastating loss only to see God use it later to help you serve others? How has he *redeemed* your pain for his purposes?

We all want that sense of significance found in achieving something bigger than just monetary or material success. Because we're eternal, spiritual beings, we yearn to create an eternal, spiritual legacy. . . . Knowing your purpose is second only to knowing Christ as your Savior. When you know what you're made for, you can take your eyes off yourself and focus on serving others as God has wired you to do. Your problems seem smaller when your purpose is bigger!

WHAT'S NEXT?, PAGE 123

Dig Deeper

You don't have to wait on God to give you a signal in order to pursue spiritual growth. He wants every believer in Christ to grow in him. In fact, as Paul notes, it is a biblical mandate:

> *But to each one of us grace has been given as Christ apportioned it. . . . So Christ himself gave the apostles, the prophets, the evangelists, the pastors and teachers, to equip his people for works of service, so that the body of Christ may be built up until we all reach unity in the faith and in the knowledge of the Son of God and become mature, attaining to the whole measure of the fullness of Christ* (Ephesians 4:7, 11–13).

How has God equipped you for works of service to benefit the body of Christ? What experiences in your life have provided experience, insight, and expertise toward living out your purpose?

As you consider your current life circumstances, how closely are you living to the center of what God made you to do? If purposeful living is your target, are you in the bull's eye? Or on one of the outer rings? Or are you still aiming at your target? Explain.

What needs to happen for you to get closer to the bull's eye?

Living out your purpose will bring fulfillment in your life. As you reflect on this, how content would you say you are in your present season? How much joy, satisfaction, and peace are you presently experiencing based on knowing and living out your purpose?

What needs to change for you to experience more freedom to serve as God created you to uniquely serve?

Who are the key people in your life whom God has used to help you see, embrace, and exercise your purpose? When has God used you to help others see their purpose more clearly?

What does spiritual maturity look like in your life? How would you finish this statement: "I would consider myself a mature Christian if _____." What role does your purpose play in your growth and maturity?

. . . .

I'm convinced that the secret to solving our problems isn't to solve them. Even if we solve one problem, another is sure to take its place. The real secret to solving problems is to have something bigger in your life, something greater and more meaningful than any earthly problem. You're welcome to keep trying to solve your problems your way. But the real solution is found in God's way. True happiness is found in purpose.

WHAT'S NEXT?, PAGE 124

. . . .

Identify

If you want to share God's love with others and help them understand the changes he can make in their lives, you first have to recognize the difference God is making *in your own life*. The following questions from chapter 9 in *What's Next?* can help you take a personal inventory of all that God is presently doing in your life. As you review each question, ask the Holy Spirit to reveal the areas where you need to reassess and redirect your time, focus, and energy.

Faith life: *How is my relationship with God?*

Marriage life: *How is my relationship with my spouse?*

Family life: *How are my relationships with my kids and immediate family?*

Work life: *How much time do I spend there, and is it effective?*

Computer life: *How can I productively spend less time on it?*

Ministry life: *How can I touch the lives of others? In what areas do I give?*

Financial life: *How are my personal finances?*

Social life: *When am I spending time engaged with friends?*

Attitudinal life: *Overall, what's my attitude lately?*

Creative life: *Am I dreaming? Writing? Creating?*

Travel life: *How do I balance time away from home and church?*

Physical life: *Am I taking care of my body and physical self?*

· · · · · · · · · · · · · · · · · · ·

There's no such thing as a small player in God's eyes. We're all teammates. Everybody is needed—which means if you don't contribute, we all suffer. Every task is vital to the work to further God's kingdom. The Bible reminds us, "All of you together are Christ's body, and each of you is a part of it" (1 Corinthians 12:27 NLT).

WHAT'S NEXT?, PAGE 132

· · · · · · · · · · · · · · · · · · ·

Take a Step

What is one God-given dream or goal you've had to put on hold due to family responsibilities, your work schedule, lack of resources, or some other obstacle? What is one step you could take to rekindle your dream and see if God wants you to pursue it?

After praying about your next step, share it with someone from your group before your next meeting. If possible, meet in person for a half hour and take turns sharing what God is revealing to you. Pray for each another as you both seek to live more fully rooted in your divine purpose.

In preparation for session 5, read the opening for section 4, "Make a Difference," and chapters 10–11 in *What's Next?* Use the space below to note any key points or questions you want to share at the beginning of your next group meeting.

SESSION 5

MAKE A DIFFERENCE

God calls each of us to be an agent of his healing in a broken world. If we're willing to listen and pay attention, he reveals such opportunities every day.

CHRIS HODGES

Getting Started

Taking the next step with God requires you to *start the journey*. As you progress, you come to *know God* and *find freedom* in him. In time, you discover your purpose as God resets your goals and dreams. And as you model Christ's example in the way you love and serve others, you find you are *making a difference* in people's lives.

Of course, it won't always be easy to take these steps. At times, God will move you out of your comfort zones. You will have to fight against distractions and competing agendas. It will involve hard work. But the end result will be worth it.

At one point in Jesus' ministry, he appointed seventy-two of his followers to go ahead of him to the towns he planned to visit. He said he was sending them out as workers in the field to reap the abundant harvest of souls for God's kingdom. He gave them authority and said those who rejected their message were rejecting God. Luke tells us what happened next:

> When the seventy-two disciples returned, they joyfully reported to him, "Lord, even the demons obey us when we use your name!"
>
> "Yes," he told them, "I saw Satan fall from heaven like lightning! Look, I have given you authority over all the power of the enemy, and you can walk among snakes and scorpions and crush them. Nothing will injure you. But don't rejoice because evil spirits obey you; rejoice because your names are registered in heaven" (Luke 10:17–20 NLT).

The followers rejoiced because they *knew they were making a difference in the world*. They had been given eyes to see the spiritual condition of the places they were visiting, and as they walked in Christ's authority they saw the demons flee. But notice Jesus didn't allow them to focus on just these successes. He reminded them of the greater prize—the treasures that awaited them in their eternal home in heaven.

Today, Jesus is calling us to do the same—to go through life looking up rather than looking around. In this final session, we will see how this kind of mindset changes all of our goals and priorities . . . and results in us leading lives that truly make a difference.

Opening Discussion

Go around the group and answer the following questions:

- When your time on earth is over, what do you want people to remember the most about you? What legacy do you want to leave behind?

- Looking back at your notes, what stood out to you in your between-sessions studies that you would like to share with the group?

Video Teaching

Play the video for session 5. As you watch, use the following outline to record any thoughts, questions, or points that stand out to you.

Notes

Keep the reason *why* you need to make a difference in front of you

Keep *heaven* as your motivation for making a difference

Two principles to keep in front of you:

Your time on earth is short

You need to make the most of every opportunity

Three thoughts on how to live your life today:

Go through life looking up, not around

Give up something now for something you want later

Intentionally make a difference

Three ways to make a difference:

Intentionally share your resources

Intentionally share your time

Intentionally share Christ

Group Discussion

Take a few minutes with your group members to discuss what you just watched and explore these concepts in Scripture.

1. What are some ways that you want to make a difference in the lives of others? How do you keep that goal in front of you as you go through your day?

2. Paul notes in Ephesians 5:15–16 that you need to make the most of every opportunity to lead others to Christ. What are some opportunities God has given you recently to share the gospel? How are you making the most of those opportunities?

3. In Philippians 3:20, Paul reminds all believers that their citizenship is in heaven. How does the truth of this verse motivate the dreams and goals you pursue on this earth?

4. In Matthew 6:19–20, Jesus tells us not to store up treasures on earth but in heaven. What does this mean to you? What are some treasures you are storing up in heaven?

5. It is God's will for you to make a difference . . . but that won't happen by accident. What are some ways (in addition to what you are already doing) that you can share your time and resources with others? What challenges do you think you will face in doing this?

6. How can you be more intentional about sharing the love of Christ with others? How can you help them discover *what's next* in their lives by helping them know God, find freedom, discover their purpose, and in turn make a difference in other people's lives?

Individual Activity

Close out today's session by completing this short activity on your own.

1. Briefly review the video outline and any notes you took.

2. In the space below, write down the most significant point you took away from this session—from the teaching, activities, or discussions.

What I want to remember from this session is . . .

Closing Prayer

Go around the room and share any prayer requests you would like the group to pray about, and then pray for those requests together. As you pray, ask God to use all you have learned and experienced during this study to nourish and stimulate further spiritual growth in your life. And don't forget to give him thanks and praise for what he is doing in each of your lives!

AFTER-SESSIONS
PERSONAL STUDY

Growing up, did you mark your height on a chart to measure your progress over time? It's only natural to want to chart your physical progress . . . and the same is true of your spiritual growth. Now that you've completed the group study, this final set of questions and exercises will help you look at your progress and examine ongoing areas of development. Before you begin, read chapters 10–11 in *What's Next?*

Reflect

Spend a few minutes today in God's presence, worshiping and thanking him for how much he loves you and wants you to grow. Ask the Holy Spirit to help you see where you need to continue focusing your efforts so you can be all that God wants you to be and make a difference. Use the questions below to guide this time of reflection.

How have you grown or changed the most since you started this study? What has contributed to this progress?

What have you enjoyed the most or found the most helpful in reading *What's Next*? What difference will this insight make as you move forward in your spiritual growth?

How has your experience in the group influenced your progress? Who in the group has encouraged or inspired you the most? How will you let that person know how much he or she has blessed you?

Is there anything you know now that you didn't grasp before you started this study? How will this new insight stimulate your spiritual growth moving forward?

What do you feel is required of you to continue knowing God at a deeper level?

Steady spiritual growth keeps us focused and anchored amid the many storms of life. We don't have to be blown and tossed around by the winds and waves of changing circumstances. Our faith in God is our foundation. He is our solid rock that never moves. . . . Moreover, our growth is critical to the mission God has given us. We're part of a body. . . . If one part doesn't grow, the rest can't function well. Like the roots of the trees in an aspen grove, when we flourish, everyone else benefits. And when we flounder, others miss out on what we have to offer.

WHAT'S NEXT?, PAGES 151–152

Dig Deeper

The goal of your spiritual growth is not to make you feel better, look "holier" to those around you, or prevent you from being selfish—though all of those benefits may naturally emerge as you mature in your faith. Rather, as Jesus explained, the purpose of knowing God, finding freedom, and discovering your purpose is so you can serve and make an investment in God's kingdom. You can make a difference for eternity! God has placed each of us on earth to serve out of the abundance of all he has entrusted to us. Jesus made this clear when he explained his own purpose to his disciples:

> *Jesus called them together and said, "You know that those who are regarded as rulers of the Gentiles lord it over them, and their high officials exercise authority over them. Not so with you. Instead, whoever wants to become great among you must be your servant, and whoever wants to be first must be slave of all. For even the Son of Man did not come to be served, but to serve, and to give his life as a ransom for many" (Mark 10:42–45).*

What are some of the ways God has called you to serve those around you? How are you presently serving them?

How have you invested most of your time, energy, and money up until this point? How would you like to invest those things moving forward?

Where have you discovered the most contentment, satisfaction, and joy in serving others? (While happiness and fulfillment are not the primary goal, you will experience the most soul satisfaction when you are obeying God, growing in your knowledge and love of him, and living out your unique purpose for the benefit of others.)

What is the primary place of leadership where God presently has you serving? Is it in your home? In your division at work? In your church? In your community? How are you exercising your gifts as you serve others in this role?

If you conducted a "spiritual audit" of the resources God has entrusted to you, how are you using each one—your time, your talents, and your treasure? In which of these three do you give back to

God the most? Which one could you use for a greater investment in God's kingdom?

What do you want your spiritual legacy to be? What difference do you want your life to make for the kingdom of God?

Identify

What has been the main area of growth for you during the course of this study? Which of the four areas—knowing God, finding freedom, discovering purpose, or making a difference—has engaged you the most? How is God working in you in this particular area of your life?

Looking back over your responses and notes for each session, what stands out to you? Is there a theme or pattern emerging that may help you discover what's next for you?

Contact a person from your group this week and share the impact this study has had on you. Listen as the person shares what he or she has learned and how he or she has grown. Ask how you can encourage the other person to continue growing in his or her amazing adventure of faith. Commit to praying for each other as you also commit to making a difference.

. . . .

Jesus plainly and unapologetically called his followers to a life of servanthood. We are to be the first to act, to serve, to do what no one else is willing to do. . . . When we serve, we receive the hidden benefit of giving to others. Jesus explained, "Now that you know these things, you will be blessed if you do them" (John 13:17). Not only do we benefit from giving all we can give, but we also have the privilege of drawing closer to Christ and the example he set for us. The more we serve, the more we want to serve!

WHAT'S NEXT?, PAGES 179–180

. . . .

Take a Step

If you want to make a difference, you need to make the most of your time on earth by using your time, energy, and resources to bless others and further God's kingdom. As Jesus said:

> *Don't store up treasures here on earth, where moths eat them and rust destroys them, and where thieves break in and steal. Store your treasures in heaven, where moths and rust cannot destroy, and thieves do not break in and steal. Wherever your treasure is, there the desires of your heart will also be* (Matthew 6:19–21 NLT).

What is the priority of your heart at this moment? Instead of focusing on your own happiness, personal gain, or individual accomplishments, how can you make a difference in the lives of others by serving them, giving to them, and being part of something enormous and eternal? God has blessed you, and will continue to bless you, so you can bless others. He allows you to share in the joy that comes from giving.

As you keep all that you've learned and experienced in mind, think about what is God calling you to do *right now* to have the greatest impact for his kingdom. Then don't put it off . . . take the first step of faith *today* toward what God is calling you to do next.

May you know joy in the journey!

Leader's Guide

Thank you for leading a small group through this study! What you have chosen to do is valuable and will make a great difference in the lives of others.

What's Next is a five-session study built around video content and small-group interaction. As the group leader, think of yourself as the host of a dinner party. Your job is to take care of your guests by managing all the behind-the-scenes details so that when everyone arrives, they can just enjoy time together.

As the group leader, your role is not to answer all the questions or re-teach the content—the video, book, and study guide will do most of that work. Your job is to guide the experience and create an environment where people can process, question, and reflect—not receive more instruction.

Make sure everyone in the group gets a copy of the study guide. This will keep everyone on the same page and help the group experience run smoothly. If some group members are unable to purchase the guide, arrange it so that people can share the resource with other group members. Giving everyone access to all the material will position this study to be as rewarding as possible. Everyone should feel free to write in their study guides and bring them to group every week.

Setting Up the Group

As the group leader, you'll want to create an environment that encourages sharing and learning. A church sanctuary or formal classroom may not be as ideal as a living room, because those locations can feel formal and less intimate. No matter what setting you choose, provide enough comfortable seating for everyone, and, if possible, arrange the seats in a semicircle so everyone can see the video easily. This will make transition between the video and group conversation more efficient and natural.

Also, try to get to the meeting site early so you can greet participants as they arrive. Simple refreshments create a welcoming atmosphere and can be a wonderful addition to a group study evening. You may also want to consider offering childcare to couples with children who want to attend. Finally, be sure your media technology is working properly. Managing these details up front will make the rest of your group experience flow smoothly and provide a welcoming space in which to engage the content of *What's Next*.

Starting Your Group Time

Once everyone has arrived, it's time to begin the group. Here are some simple tips to make your group time healthy, enjoyable, and effective.

First, consider beginning the meeting with a short prayer, and remind the group members to put their phones on silent. This is a way to make sure you can all be present with one another and with God. Then, give each person one or two minutes to respond to the questions in the "First Impressions" section. You won't need much time in session 1, but beginning in session 2, people will likely need more time to share insights from their personal studies. Usually, you won't answer the discussion questions yourself, but you should go first with the "First Impressions" question, answering briefly and with transparency.

At the end of session 1, invite the group members to complete the Between-Sessions personal studies for that week. Explain that you will be providing some time before the video teaching next week for anyone to share insights. Let them know sharing is optional, and it's no problem if they can't get to some of the between-sessions activities some weeks. It will still be beneficial for them to hear from the other participants and learn about what they discovered.

During the "First Impressions" section, help the members who completed the personal studies debrief their experiences. Debriefing something like this is a bit different from responding to questions based on the video, because the content comes from the participants' real lives. The basic experiences that you want the group to reflect on are:

- *What was the best part about this week's personal study?*
- *What was the hardest part?*
- *What did I learn about myself?*
- *What did I learn about God?*

There is a specific question written to help process each activity, but feel to expand on this time or adapt the questions based on the dynamics of your group.

Leading the Discussion Time

Now that the group is engaged, it's time to watch the video and respond with some directed small-group discussion. Encourage all the group members to participate in the discussion. As the discussion progresses, you may want to follow up with comments such as, "Tell me more about that," or, "What helped you come to that conclusion?" This will allow the group participants to deepen their reflections and invite meaningful sharing in a welcoming way.

Note that you have been given multiple questions to use in each session, and you do not have to use them all or even follow them in order. Feel free to pick and choose questions based on either the needs of your group or how the conversation is flowing. Also, don't be afraid of silence. Offering a question and allowing up to thirty seconds of silence is okay. It allows people space to think about how they want to respond and also gives them time to do so.

As group leader, you are the boundary keeper for your group. Do not let anyone (yourself included) dominate the group time. Keep an eye out for group members who might be tempted to "attack" folks they disagree with or try to "fix" those having struggles. These kinds of behaviors can derail a group's momentum, so they need to be steered in a different direction. Model active listening and encourage everyone in your group to do the same. This will make your group time a safe space and create a positive community.

The group discussion time leads to a closing individual activity. During this time, encourage the participants to take just a few minutes to review what they've learned and write down two key takeaways. This will help them cement the big ideas in their minds as you close the session. Close your time together with prayer as a group.

Thank you again for leading your group. You are making a difference!

ALSO AVAILABLE FROM CHRIS HODGES

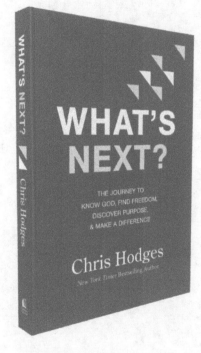

Available wherever books
and ebooks are sold.

Printed in the USA
CPSIA information can be obtained
at www.ICGtesting.com
LVHW030713050824
787165LV00011B/150

9 780310 104124